Card,

Maybe, the only thing
that we need to build a
home is a floor, where we
can sit down together ?
· Chat.
Love you lots!
Graziella

PRAISE FOR
KAY ULANDAY BARRETT

"Kay's command of craft, commitment to truth, and dedication to art as service is to be commended. I believe that Kay is an artist of merit. Kay is all heart. All in. We need Kay's stories, Kay's stellar art, Kay's warrior vision."

> – **Sharon Bridgforth**, author of *love conjure/blues* and the Lambda Literary Award-winning *the bull-jean stories*

"These poems are songs–aching, beautiful, necessary songs that transport and transform."

> – **Eli Clare**, author of *Exile and Pride* and *Brilliant Imperfection: Grappling with Cure*

"[Kay's poetry is] embodied, thick and fluid. Read them with your body and spirit on notice."

> – **Alexis Pauline Gumbs**, author of *Spill: Scenes of Black Feminist Fugitivity* and *M Archive: After the End of the World*

More Than Organs
Copyright © 2020 by Kay Ulanday Barrett

Cover art: *Stars Samuel de Champlain Park* by Kyle Wong
        A real human heart inside a jar by Camilo Jimenez

Cover collage and design by Seth Pennington

Author photograph by Jess X. Chen

Sibling Rivalry Press, LLC
PO Box 26147
Little Rock, AR 72221

info@siblingrivalrypress.com

www.siblingrivalrypress.com

ISBN: 978-1-943977-74-1

Library of Congress Control No. 2019953147

By special invitation, this title is housed in the Rare Book and Special Collections Vault of the Library of Congress.

First Sibling Rivalry Press Edition, March 2020

MORE THAN ORGANS

KAY ULANDAY BARRETT

SIBLING RIVALRY PRESS
DISTURB/ENRAPTURE
LITTLE ROCK, ARKANSAS

For everybody who sat on my stoop on Whipple St. and especially for my tita, Yolanda Salvo and lolo, Guillermo Ulanday. Thank you for making home. Thank you for believing this scrappy brown kid with big glasses could be a writer and an artist when everybody else tried to turn them into somebody else. Here's some words that would've never been possible without you.

For all the Brown, Queer, Transgender, and Non-Binary People who are Sick, Disabled, Depressed, and Alive. For the kindred we've lost. For those in the future, I'm holding you with me.

Mahal: a prologue

Isa: *one*

Dalawa: *two*

Tatlo: *three*

Apat: *four*

Mahal
a prologue

in tagalog, the term **mahal** is a
noun and translates to *love*.
however, as an adjective it means
expensive or *costly* or *overpriced* or
dear or *beloved* or *cherished* or *valued*.

this word is shifted in meaning
by tone, context, cadence. the word
becomes interchangeable, durable.
like an imposed tongue. like a pushed
out community. like forced migration.
like being raised in the hood.
like what it means to leave everything.
like what it means to survive most things.

there's a way the word becomes
all of the things at the same time.
not so much a double entendre,
more like different routes, traveling
along the same curve of body.

everything is at the expense
of this word.

**this book is for all of those who
know the breadth of this word:**

mahal, n.
> love

mahal, adj.
> expensive

11

Isa: one

Tibo

after Gloria Anzaldúa

A child isn't so much
a discovery
but a dragging.

Rene F. is informed
that you are
in fact
in love with her.

Joseph Pinkett found a love letter
you wrote and stole it, gave it to her.

She kisses you in the basement
after CCD class for approximately
six minutes
six lifetimes
six laps in kilometers

or miles
or basically,
your mouth feels like
$\qquad\qquad$ galaxy.

Thumbs
become bruises after signing
the cross so many times.
Fair exchange.

Forward
$\qquad$ Still refuse anything
$\qquad$ but shorts and pants.

$\qquad$ Scraped knees from a
$\qquad$ belly kick
$\qquad$ telling you,
$\qquad\qquad$ *be a girl*
$\qquad\qquad$ *BE A GIRL*

Forward

> you crave that 1.5-inch gap between the skirt
> and whatever happens between inner thighs.
>
> The.   Gap.
>
> Sylvia was the first girl to take you there,
> where   you   stayed.
> You never wanted to leave.

Forward

> Kicked out
> spat at
> > *YOU are not my child!*
>
> Found making out with the first real girlfriend.
> Here, learn kissing can be mistaken for bloodletting.
>
> Your mama turned anything that
> belonged to you into
> a weapon.
>
> Whole hopes
> thrashed to dust.

Forward

> Reconciliation
> is a mother who
> refuses to look you in the eye.
>
> In response,
> you move food to the tenor
> of small talk
> you are terrible at.

Forward

Only talk about meals
—how the crab was,
did the fish need more salt?
Treaties signed by taste buds.

You plan vacation the same time as
mama goes back home
sa Pilipinas.

Remember:
during your final goodbye
—you didn't know that then—
she swells up in your hands.

It's as though all of her becomes
blanket or dough. After this,
you never see her again.

Forward

The next time she
arrives to greet you,
accept the ashes.

Aunties love it when seafood is on sale

Argyle Redline, Chicago, IL / After Giselle Buchanan

In summertime, the women
in my family spin sagoo
like planets, make
even Saturn blush.
They split leaves
of kang kong with
riverbed softness.

They are precise;
measure rice by palm lines
with laughter and season
broth made of last gasps.
You'd swear they were
teenagers again, talk gossip
stretch limbs
elastic, durable, like seaweed.

Come dinner time,
skilled mouths slurp
through the domes of
shrimp and crab.

They
prize the fat—

the angles of their teeth
splinter claw, snap sinew,
dip tart into sweet
then back again
bitterness balanced,
succulence on succulence,
is to find flesh from the
smallest of spaces.

Women
who swallow whole,
make a pile of bones,
suck teeth,
taste every morsel,
so that all that is left
is a quiet room
and shells of what once was.

To the daughters
of dried fish nets
whose dreams dragged on sand,
dragged to this country,
they bring home recipes years later,
flick joints to garlic,
salabat to the sick,
culinary remix, teach cousins
this is how we stay alive,
—mourning in the Midwest
by taste bud.

Afterwards, they keep the ocean
husks for another meal
because to get a good deal
is to double.
Anybody from the island
will tell you,
that is where the true flavor is

and what is hunger
anyway, but the carving
out of emptiness,
the learning to always
save something
for later?

For tita idna, tita yoly, tita chit, & lola rita

Right to release

For the longest time, I dreaded bathrooms,
the bleach singeing nostrils, I pictured my brown mama
in every white person's house, scrubbing tile,
making what other people took
for granted, shine.

In airports, I clench my bladder.
In public anywhere, I hold it until a 3rd floor walk up can turn bloody.

There's a story every trans person mouths when they have to pee.
It's not in the bladder but guttural, it goes like this:

I am real. I am real. I am real. Shit, I really gotta go!

If what they say is true,
that bathrooms are where we are all most human,
than I am a dilapidated national geographic,
barely mammal, told to leave in the dirtiest of places.

Example:
[brown girl lowers her register like it's of cobwebs & steel, slouches in
a baggy shirt, goes beeline for the stall. doesn't want to wash her hands,
because he'll have to scrape off the stares in daydreams   the next day and
the next, til their girlfriend's hands make pillows because in your dreams,
they could still get your pronouns wrong.]

Next:
                they are told as a boi that they are in the wrong place.
                To drink a cup of water is a hazard in waiting.

Honestly, I wish we could
just shit on every curse, on every time
some Trans woman turns threat when she just wants
a mirror to see herself in full-length glory.

Once a month, I want to announce shark week & build a
structure of blood that would make Rapunzel shiver and
take the crimson to write (because ALL good poets, we
just LOVE the word "CRIMSON")

I am real. I am real. I am real.

You do not have to punch it out of me,
a bruised eye like a swollen gourd.
A kicked rib the density of a smashed plum.
      Do you know how long it takes for me to accept a hug?

Here is my blood.
Its sacrilege ascends the repellent stares.
For hormones or not, I am no waste-of-time dumping ground
to let your terrors that haunt
you in a whisper
(((((SPOILER ALERT)))))
      guess what, YOU aren't normal, or real either.

The locker room hush,
the road trip bus stop stink,
the fast food restaurant stain,

forgive me, we know how this story ends.
But do we?

Is it so wrong to want to clench your jaw in the light,
praise any shape of chest in the fluorescents,
catalogue an altar from my hips to the new hair on the chin,
sit alone on the throne in leisure,
not headline,
not gravestone,
not hash tag,
not ash.

Though I am never clean, I'm not ever going to be,
your colonization that forced my family here
made sure of that,
but what I do know is this:
           a brown woman & child
           cannot grow in your shit.

Can I just feel the water from the tap
on my knuckles like baptism?
Because we as humans are 60% water
and though I am never clean,
let me tell you,
the tide of ocean beats inside me.
Have you ever tried to contain a wave
or date a water sign?

No matter what,
nothing   nothing
can take away
its right to release.

song for the kicked out & weary

after Sonia Sanchez

the streets are not paved with gold, they lied.
I got a rough throat, I got a rough life.

The streets are not paved with gold, they lied.
I got too much queer in me to live their way tonight.

She found me waist up in you.
My mama found me mouthful, drinkin' you.

Mama said that I was the devil, made this journey here a waste,
couldn't I be more American?
Couldn't I just wear dresses, wear lipstick, make money,

anak, it's so hard in this country, please
couldn't I just behave?

mama said *leave this house!* Her spirit filled with ache.
All my belongings freckled the streets
I slept outside, my journey is not self-made.

I say all you laughin' & jukin' in the alleys.
I say all you sleepin' to roach cries.
I say all you couch surfin' until the next night.
I say all you kissin' despite the fists and fights.

Together we are a prayer, no matter what.
Together we are an anthem despite their hetero fuss.
Together we are stronger than the world's unsaids.
Together we are as mighty as our ancestors up from the dead.

We are bigger than the skylines that hold us.
We are bigger than the sirens that stab our hearts.
We are bigger than the talk of boystown progress, rainbow flags, & bars.
We are bigger than bleeding our blood to the stars.

Together we are a prayer, no matter what.
Together we are an anthem despite their hetero fuss.
Together we are stronger than the world's unsaids.
Together we are as mighty as our ancestors up from the dead.

More than organs

A person is more than organs, more than skin cell flecks
on bed sheets when your whole Monday is fading
away, out of breath.

The average person breathes seven hundred million breaths in a lifetime, but
what happens when each one might taste of blades, pills, between havoc and
delirium, an inhale can carve you out when you are all alone. I sometimes
think I am beyond statistics and that life is a trapdoor.

I think I collect knotted rust from bridges in my feet.
I bet, warped twine is on search party somewhere
just waiting to keep me together.

What do you say to limbs when they are good friends with scalpels?
When you feel your insides grate through chemicals like a marathon with no
winner? When the only metal comes from you, hours of bleeding creatures
you have no names for, how do you answer those texts messages that ask
How are you doing?

It's the salt, stained smell of iron. Sea of your body is
a wave that makes it impossible to stand. The body is a letter
folded backwards, all strange angles, confessions
bleeding through the surface. Like this, I am something
that feels like it'll always be there but
manages to get lost somehow.

If I told you that my life is basically cloud cover,
between shade and safe haven,
between starling and storm, you'd get why each cough
is the split broken back
of a palm tree, why my own palms

hold out to the air and

say   *hello*
say   *I missed you*
say   *please stay with me here*
say   *please stay with me*
say   *please stay*

                                  please.

pain, an epistle

you never asked for this. that's the truth,
but like all your people, your cane is a
drum-song and you're no stranger to
bullshit. what stories does your blood
tell? we could say, howl, say part limping
tree and part starlight. we could say that
you're a survivor of systems that stretch
you out broader than any creature of
wingspan can imagine. never mind,
the destruction, the parched throat, the
pill cocktails, the *sorry, there are stairs*.
adversity is a jigsaw of stethoscopes,
racism, whatever people think a real lady
should be. you are slow, babyboi. you are
okay. you are worthwhile of expanse. let
them all fucking wait; you are breathing.
remember, the best stuff takes time to
simmer, ruminate, to sit in the shape of
things. your allies: bed, wakeful sunrise,
peanut butter by said bed, heating pad,
sometimes a lover, only sometimes.
when they ask you, *where have you
gone?* ask instead, *why haven't you stayed?*
when you can't do lighthearted small talk
at events you can hardly make it to after
all, your nerves rampant screamers, this
means your body in itself is a protest and
placard. what is more anti-empire? what
is more bounty? do not fool yourself
that everyone will understand the
wonder of this, moreover, the draining
of it. blessed is the stranger who watches
you cough and doesn't flinch. blessed
is the cloudscape greeting you at the
windowsill for the 3rd or 6th day in a
row from your mattress view. holy is the
wolf howl of joints that murmur to a
lull under right temperature. holy is just
living living living or trying to.

Notes from Brown People in Mackinaw City, MI.

> "The longest running free Memorial Day historical program in U.S. takes places for the 50th year in Mackinaw City: the Fort Michilimackinac Historical Reenactment Pageant, the three-day pageant that brings to life the 1763 Fort Michilimackinac battle between the French, British, and Native Americans."

> — visitmackinawcitymichigan.com

During the first year of college, a perky Korean girl finagles the hair of a quiet blonde boy and denounces, *Filipinos are NOT real Asians*. Flashback: your mama whose curly hair isn't straightened enough for kung-fu flicks or the Chinatown lady at a register who, due to this fact, overcharges for crab. Ma wants the best bargain, so she would pull her hair back to a bun, so maybe nobody could tell, all the curls.

+

We started in rural Michigan, her side jobs doing manicures for bored blue-eyed housewives as the #2 Avon sale rep of the county. The sound of files sanding down talons, her song. As the half-blood born into a nebulous island hum, my hands were sticky with wild raspberries. I'd only heard of mango, of lychees, then. This is what happens when you are away from your own people, even familiar turns fiction.

+

During town re-enactments, my mom and I never had the choice to be pilgrims. No bonnets. No aprons. No stone roofs for us. *You don't even need to paint your face!* An organizer would inform us. Here, I imply that we were Brown already and there were possibly white people who painted their faces, never getting our color right.

+

Us two, the only other Brown people in moccasins. The Pottawatomie and Ottawa peoples, all with long black braids adorning their shoulders, the colonials in red jackets prompting all of us, *when you hear the cannons, you run! Got that?* My mother never said a word. Sat there, quiet with the other Brown women. Even after the boom, my mother would instruct me to stay put.

+

Once, when mom's co-worker bellowed across the room, *You're from Mexico, right?* both our gazes couldn't lift from the ground. We became that patch of silence where two people who don't have the same perspective look to the sky or the ground for answers.

+

Which brings me to this: What is it to come from an invisible place, when even your nation is unnamed and yet, funny story—you're still somehow able to breathe?

Origin Story for my chest or whatever it was

what I'd give to tell you your arc was acceptable,
sprouted at age nine, every man on the street clocked you
and what was a girl, **folded** arms over every rounded part.

a child could hide away, but everyone knew
there was supposedly a woman underneath.

as a teenager, you would squint as the barrage of grade school
silhouettes just reminded me of strangers, dead names,
a graveyard of off-kilter smiles. each face, somewhere else,
each face asking for their bodies to vanish.

you grow into a tomboy on their knees.
by this time, a schoolyard scraped you with chants,
Girl or boy! Girl or boy!

I know you never understood which to choose
so you stayed there, close to the ground like prayer,
as cruel jokes gathered what was left.

a teacher reported a black eye
and a suspension. no culprits. just your body
a punishment
of itself,
a thing you
hardly even believed.

remember this moment, you
out of breath, pleading.

this will not be the first time
you will be told you deserve to be alone
for being who you are.

not the first time
curled up
in your own orbit,
a curse for every curve.

On departure & how to say goodbye to your chest

I give my chest a pep talk,
an (un)grateful farewell.

It's not a talking to, just resolution.
It's a basic goodbye.

The kind of honorable glare you
give a worthy opponent, a cordial enemy,

you know they are in the room but you
ignore their good graces, their attempts to
become a part of your life.
They never get you anyway.

At best, they are a family member you
acknowledge between battles

where love
isn't exactly the word
you'd ever use.

Love, artifact

The air is a thicket or jar of jam.
We're breathing in bulbous catastrophe but with
layers of plexiglass over our faces, *breathing*
      is a loose word. Shit, wearing masks
     used to be
          a fashion statement, not need.

When they kiss you for the first time, masks
are off. There are only 3 hours of free space air for us
a day. This is what you choose to do with it:

Get wet like the ancestors before us,
         fumble hair strands
      in eager crooks of palms,
make a garden of the minute,
bury your heart in the mud,
         make your pulse   bigger.

It wasn't always this way.
Lovers could sufficiently waste one
another's time on the last planet.
This is what old newspaper headlines state.
    Bumbling lungs that didn't have to beg for air.

Plants used to be our source, corals made way for
more minutes. Oxygen of earth from earth.
                  That was then.

On this dome, we sneak glances over love interests
in aluminum. Save up our devotion in moments.
We can't be remarkable in our eruptions like our grandparents.

Spontaneity is fossil. Fingertips have long
    forgotten the concept of kinetic.

Why did we let it get to this point—

God what *would* you do if they just touched
your cheek without planning to?

A new life they promised us. One better after the climate
stopped grappling with our mistakes. We made far
too many, and now to kiss is a daydream thing.

Love,
Artifact.

Please—
Take off your helmet.
Welcome the storm.

We can learn to breathe again or
let us just cherish this air,
let us inhale even it breaks us for trying.

actually, jenny schecter wasn't the worst...

but you know who was? doesn't matter how political the
room, somebody usually will always mention *The L Word*
and OH MY GOD SHANE is the hot. H-O-T—hottest EVER.
OMFG. still. it is 2018 & white desire leans up against
a wall, says zero words, leaves the brown woman at the
altar, but *there was depth there, there was depth there.*
HBO gifted the lesbian world the original fuckboi—

cum, see how white mediocrity finger fucks! by that, I mean:
fucks you over. look, we lesbians can be normal jerks too.
closer to fine. closer to whitened aspirations. i know what
you're about to say: *her character was. so. misunderstood.*
waaaaaas it, though? misunderstood is not the same as standardized
desire. misunderstood is an order at starbucks, when one
receives a grande as opposed to a venti.   hotness is not
misunderstood. there is a schematic diagram of expectations

& apparently, year 2003 is still standard? hotness
is a latina character played by a desi woman played a fool
by a white woman as brown & black women only have sex
together in jail cells, in heated passion, behind bars as fantasy.
never seen again. somebody said, yes this is a good idea,
pan to the white woman being *so sorry* again—I know,
I know we need representation. who's we? currently, there is
only one show on air in 2018 that depicts two women of color

who love each other on screen. what's a body when it has
never witnessed love from their own? contrary to belief,
I think for every time we don't experience two brown
girls enveloped in a gaze at a bar, at the school dance, in the gym,
at the coffee shop, on the stoop, in the hood, in a car, making
breakfast, listening to blues, humming kundimans, we accept normal,
turn to irreverent dust, forget what we are, forget we are enough.
for getting away with shame every channel—our hearts remote,
passions on pause, view hers growing up to be something never given
the chance   how you gonna know what joy is if even the
prospect of a kiss together is canceled   every damn time?

Spasm: a personal ethnography
and then, I thought about Cayden Clarke*

1.

S/he/dead name's medical reports that spasms happen only during:

> "a walk to the market, going to a concert, this loss
> shucking rasp, the empire, awkward first dates,
> anything colonial really, the buzz of a big big crowd,
> under 30 degrees F., when someone politely asks your
> name, laugh in mid-joke, humidity from the rain, the
> thought of tinder even for 5 seconds, pocked moments
> of shame."

2.

(are you okay? it's okay. are you okay? it's okay. you're beautiful, you're
beautiful. YOU are beautIFul. you are beautiFUL where are you now? stay
here with me? you are here with me. let me hold you? hold you. hold you.
ssshhhhhh. you're HANDsome. want to describe it to me? what do you need?
magical starlight. beautiful comet. let's create a safe word when this happens,
okay? come here. shhhh. sexy. it's okay. it's okay. we can stop.)

3.

Wince. Portal to not here.
To explain it, it's about
performance & about thresholds.
Every trip to anywhere is staggered drag.
Cue: Well-behaved token. Flightless bird. *Fuck,*
I couldn't make the deadline/that class/this interview
because… Cue: Bootstraps don't apply here. My parents
worked so hard to get to this country so…*Cue: Super Crip. Cue:*
Look them in the eyes, that's how they know you are "paying attention."
Question whatever wholeness means, full, unabashed, span. Our parents came
on boats / after partition / fled the dictator / on asylum, so…Are they staring?
Do they know it's happening right now? *Cue: Homogenous understand-*
ings of community. Let them stare. It happens all the time. Jagged
face scrawl, spit drawl daring. *Oh, I am sorry you couldn't*
make it, maybe next time? Cue: The goal is to be just
like everyone else. FB EVENT reads: This event
is standing room only. Guess it's just you &
Netflix tonight. Remember, stethoscope &
clipboard are corroborators. Who's at the
door? *Cue: No, wait, officer, wait—*
what, I can't stop. This is
just how my
bod—

* [1] Unnamed Arizona police officers shot to death a 24-year-old transgender man in his own home on Thursday, according to a report from *ABC 15 Arizona.* (*The Advocate*).

[2] Clarke, an Autistic Transgender white man who lived with suicidal ideation and PTSD who, during a police visit to his home, was murdered (Me).

Dalawa: two

(Jungle Asian)

nanay used to make a toothpick of fish bone after cleaning out cheeks next to gills, *the softest tastiest part!* aunties chime in like we was on camera or some shit (Jungle Asian) domestic workers in the background of the big Asian movie who look downward but send their kids money for books (Jungle Asian) check the tags on the t-shirts, swap sale tags like the way we swapped names to get here (Jungle Asian) lola makes necklace by petals of sampaguita together like she's just stepped on sand (Jungle Asian) coconut oil on brown skin, hair, any snack ever (Jungle Asian) brown like baked pandesal fresh from the oven, not no light mother of pearl (Jungle Asian) spam for breakfast (Jungle Asian) rosary beds as back up phone call, a cross on the breath of chest bone, remember—we weren't asked here, we were forced here, invitations don't clean up people's bile or ungrateful children or are told they are part of the family when they ain't seen their real blood or banana leaves in years (Jungle Asian) *tell you what*—tito says, as he misses a sentence to recall his smashed face on ground, machine gun cracks his name into skull still (Jungle Asian) mahjong big win means new shoes for everybody, a black label whiskey shot to remind us even our triumph stings (Jungle Asian).

*

means naks - *you look good!* ay nako - *an element of surprise!* means brown knuckles on white boys faces on schoolyard concrete for saying *ew! bet your family eats dogs!?* (Jungle Asian) balisong safety unhinged, as double blade as your tongue taught to pirouette, grace air with such shimmer nobody ever sees that attack or insult coming (Jungle Asian) that starter jacket hustle (Jungle Asian) that calling card shuffle (Jungle Asian) that honda civic slow stroll come spring time we can hear two blocks away (Jungle Asian) that sleeve of ink on your arm because your people are waves & snake skin, means we take thorns of calamansi, prick ourselves with both the tart & sharp, make our celebration ritual some kinda psychological struggle (Jungle Asian) that too casual clarification over which war, *when Spain came &... when Japan came &... when America never left. what year did China..? ... did the French ever? ... Is that why we like baguettes?*

*

(Jungle Asian) hello, my name is (Jungle Asian) I wiped up tables, coyly carved freedom from cops like my ancestors with machete, my ancestors out on weekend nights pressed in zoot suits about to be hand cuffs, like every pop n' lock, every crew with sleeves rolled up to balance the gravity against their bodies. (Jungle Asian) maybe the world is wild out there, but my people have cackled when bombs made blossoms, carried beats in their hips as the carnage came (Jungle Asian) my dear people (Jungle Asian) make constellations of ball gowns in the most remote of provinces pushed out to Tampa, DC, LA, Chicago, New Orleans. my bading & bakla titas sparkle, put blush on before & after the storm comes. they stay glorious. (Jungle Asian) tell us fire is made for killing and we'll show you a dance floor (Jungle Asian) in any neighborhood where elders can't help but do the electric slide on a saturday, cuz all they got for one another, for this life, for at least this one song, is shine shine shine (Jungle Asian).

consider the gender spectrum

"I know what it is to be broken and be bold
Tell you that my silver is gold"
— Moses Sumney

when all your skin / reads trespass / reads not worth a piss /
literally / reads not even worth excrement / reads good enough to not be
dead / maybe if she sleeps with me / i am trained to think / pity

once / a man spat in my face / kicked / my cane / touched his
dick like a small itch / i erased into words like / dyke she-man die die /
you're never going to be / real / he says

as i was saying / another dude pushed me / stalked me for blocks until
i turned the corner / and faked a call on my / cell phone
that guy said / you don't have any friends / and he wasn't wrong exactly

i am not a real man / this doesn't happen to / everybody's right
to be real / doesn't mean a war to meet someone's / parents or
to wear a shirt at the mall / because what is your love / but shame / worthy

this world / makes me feel that way / no matter the / constellation
of well-intentioned quotes / or rainbow-like buttons / no words can be barrier /
for night terrors so i make / like a flicker / smile at parties / which is a lie really

for wanting / to be here / which is the scapegoat / of something
larger / says my therapist / and he quotes me throwing fire / back
to my heart / when all I want is to be melted / not almost ashes /

another dark poem / says another editor / and i think
this is nothing / i have a therapist at least / picture an alley / where
your legs are tangled to / dumpster groans / and if actually reported on

the news / they jam you between a funny bird story / and a partly sunny
forecast / and for fifteen seconds the anchor / doesn't blink and
bet you / they get your name wrong / again / hash tag here

What one does after poetry reading at the hotel

You stay long after the last poem,
thank the janitor whose face
is your cousin's face.

Say: *Sir, you should take this food home.*
As he shyly smiles, you nudge,
*My mom would bring me these square
cheeses, after her late night cleaning shifts.
didn't even know to pronounce them then.*

His face softens, as you make him a tower of a plate.
Think of Tito Jun who ate strawberries
and camembert like a secret king.
Think of cousins Joy and Jane who would
sword fight cocktail toothpicks. Bright
cellophane tails, fake bursts of blood.

You wrap up the dish the way women
taught you, watch staff hover over
a table in disarray—divvy up mozzarella,
broken cracker corners, vegetables
just good enough for the next day.

In your world,
treasure has always had
an expiration date.

*

Years of platters from parties
where your loved ones
were never looked
in the eye. How you were raised
on scraps, acquired taste for brie
as much as your resentment for
people who threw napkins in
the faces of your elders.

Here you are,
special guest, honored speaker,
Bong, leader of servers
is relaxed, top button undone.
Rosary beads burst
from under throat.

It could be whiskey or release of
responsibility   maybe both.
Asks me
where my family is from,
when have I gone back
I'm so sorry about your nanay,
is it just you? At least, she could go home…

Everyone takes pause,
caterers, servers, custodial staff.
People who are told they
can't afford to stop,
felt suspended in air.
He means *for the last time,*
she didn't die here,
bend body over again,
die feeding strangers,
take food that wasn't hers.

*

We smile far,
like we're reaching for
coconut rinds though
we stand in Ballroom H
in the midwest December.
By the end of the night,
I take my baon, my poems,
words folded in half, inward like
they are rocking
themselves
to sleep.

Earthbenders are Black and Brown Girls

For Elizabeth

Between her toes, fingers, earth split,
worm warm, blades of grass
lilted on summer sneakers.
She was in love.

In small town Minnesota, there's the face of someone
who'll embrace her name years later,
but for now the grit of soil is epiphany.
Bark, an experiment.

Nobody gets up with the sun in her house.
Slow faces half awake, spring and leave
as she's squeezing mulberries.

Streaks of juice sheen on palms, paint of
saccharine and root, by afternoon,
honeysuckle in her hair.

A moving forest, she'd laugh herself until dirt
streaked beneath fingernails.
Earth-song on everything
she touched.

She would scale blocks,
a pebble in a satchel,
a turned-over stone,
fingers like antennae plowing caverns.

No doubt
that if she pressed
her cheek against the ground,
she swore it
lived.

Swore
it moved.

People say that we've survived Reagan

Trump Inauguration, January 2017

And I am sick of that
shit
—Then, do explain
my mama's
wails

like purge on childhood
or folded
envelopes aunties
got when their
husbands

never returned
from a war
meant to
pay for college
or even the
white
gay professor pocked in scars
skin an unanticipated
forecast

who survived
the
AIDS
epidemic

or what he called
Annihilation
to a class of college students
trying to
get extra credit

You don't get it

*I'm the
only one left
alive*

Was all
he kept

saying.

Albany Park/Logan Square 1993-2000, Chicago IL.

Accents, hard A's ascending on the roof of the mouth,
angry and anticipated, assembled by the air they miss all over.

Boys brandish harsh syllables, *Don't be so bakla!*
They berate. They break. They belittle.
Brraaap braaap baraaap   making fake
bullets into one another's brows.

Crips and Disciples. Color-clad clothing.
Categorize blocks / careful cartography.

Did I mention deep fryer sizzle as shrimp heads popPOP with scallions, garlic,
adobo peppercorns flicker oil like summer afternoon jump rope sessions?

Elegance is a dozen expectant elders roving through a bbq,
          for balut, halo halo brazenly melted onto soft oblong
                    palms which is basically as good as prayer.

The Filipino's first call and response:
          Kain na tayo! Time to eat! Food is ready! Get your asses ovah here, na!

Guaranteed commentary by a gaggle of aunties—*Ganda, no?!*
gasped over the grass. At the same time, ghosts on ghosts on maws
of lolas who gesture with rosaries.

Look, to plastic bags heaped in hands, *can you hold this for me, child?*

Inquiries like furtive urban inquisition:
                    So when are you going to college?
                    Where is your boyfriend?
                    Did you know—insert name—is pregnant?
                              going to the army?
                              ran away?
                              was locked up?

Jackfruit in spoonfuls. Jaded by the roomfuls. Jalopy speakers croon choruses of
Sharon Cuneta.

Kids linked together summer nights like split sutures / their insides spill,
sanctify the sidewalk. What's caution when there's kindred?

Lolo: *Look, take these flowers to your mama.*
  Say they are from the both of us.

Miscreant: noun, [mis-kree-uh nt]
  (Migrant. Misplaced. Mapping. Misunderstood. Melancholy. Mahirap.)

Naturally, the bone cracks are from neighbors rushing to their night shifts,
their packed lunches in knapsacks with a nest for feet.

I captured glow bugs / butts blinking / a collection of cosmos,
OHHHH Hoy! What you doing?! You cannot keep creatures too long contained,
they'll lose their shine!!

I would eat ice cream for breakfast.
PP AA HH LLLL EEETT AAAAHHH!
Pulp packed   on popsicle sticks,   papaya, pinya,

Quezon City twang still sticks even after decades in America.

Roosters as alarm clocks rake the sky.

Stoop stunners, all of us. Family be like, sacred songs sung from old
homelands.
We be sand daydreamers to stay alive in this country.

"Till tomorrow, I'll be holding you tight
And there's nowhere in the world I'd rather be
Than here in my room dreaming about you and me."
                                        – Selena.

Upswing.
Upset.

Vexed parents as another police officer pounds the
                        hips of doors til they drill whatever out of you.

YO! Was that Tita Yoly yanking up the weeds on Albany and Waveland,
in her tropical flower moomoo? It ain't the kang kong of her riverbed,

but it will have to do.

Exhaustion or Exclusion, for instance.

Yawning young ones
yammer to cross the street,   *You got your homework?*

Sometimes indistinguishable with "S"
as in *selos* (pronounced like *zelos*),
as in jealousy.
As in what's supposed to consume you
              when   you grow up   from   nothing.

While looking at photo albums
Christmas Eve, 2016

Before everyone died—in my family—first definition I
learned was—my mother's maiden name, ULANDAY—
which literally means—of the rain—and biology books
remind us—pouring has a pattern—has purpose—namesake
means release—for my mother meant, flee—meant leave—
know exactly what parts of you—slip away—drained
sediment of a body—is how a single mama feels—on the
graveyard shift—only god is awake—is where my—family
banked itself—a life rooted in rosaries—like nuns in
barricade—scream—People Power—one out of five—leave
to a new country—the women in my family hone—in my
heart—like checkpoints—which is what they know—which
is like a halt—not to be confused for—stop—which is what
happened to my ma's breath—when she went home—for
the last time—I didn't get to—hold her hand as she died—I
said I tried—just translates to—I couldn't make it—in
time—I tell myself—ocean salt and tear salt—are one and
the same—I press my eyes shut—cup ghost howl—cheeks
splint wood worn—which is to say—learn to make myself a
harbor—anyway—once I saw a pamphlet that said—what to
do when your parent is dead—I couldn't finish reading—but
I doubt it informs the audience—what will happen—which
is to say—you will pour your face & hands—& smother your
mother's scream on everything—you touch—turn eyelids
into oars—go, paddle to find her.

Rhythm is a Dancer, again.

#ForOrlando

When the responders came to a nightclub in Orlando,
they announced *If you are still alive, raise your hand.*

Meanwhile,   I was asleep in a bed I never thought I would have.
People like us are used to lonely, are used to sobbing   so hard

that homes are like unfathomable dreams.   We search for
the rescue of safety in our own skin and reasons to just hold

someone's hand,   to just find a job that doesn't
call us by the wrong name, to just find ourselves lost in music.

Earlier that night, people didn't get to leave the dance floor.
What is the beat of bullets   when we are too used to percussion   already?

Cusses & threats beat at the seams of our skin, of course
salvation is to tut & tick on our own terms and tears are but

dance sweat so as the gunshots from the balcony seared the air,
there were boys holding hands   with other boys   for the first time

which then became their last time,   and there were others trying
to forget a hard day to the lilt of limbs, at the lip of a bottle,

there were strobe lights that could've been falling stars   but
instead   they were bodies.

Before we die,   some of us are already dead to family photos,
our own blood kin close their eyes to us like caskets.

In a club, there was a young person or three, singing aloud,
who thought   *This my favorite song,*   a palm up to the air and the only

place that was safe became barrage, glass shards, their
friend's blood now blanket.   The next morning, I couldn't stop

crying and I will tell you,   we've been crying a long time.
We've lit candles at vigils like it's as everyday as breathing.

We know the choreography of loss.   If there are no prayers possible,
understand moments before there were claps praising the dip of a harmony,

then nothing.   This isn't a shining beacon of a new reality.
There is no epiphany. Lives have always been at stake,   dance floors
have always   been altar, a song   isn't ever just   a song

In which your white doctor informs you that he worked on a Navy base in the Philippines

After Bao Phi

(Misgendered by Nurse. Puts on hospital gown. Doctor enters the room, shakes your hand to greet you. Misgenders you, again. Swings feet on the exam table. Kicks the air. Kicks air. Kicks air.)

---

* feels like calling an older sister, Baby / feels like Baby is now first name for hundreds of women because that is what soldiers called women in my country, which means getting women ready for something / feels like wanting to fuck grown woman with payment of an American candy bar / feels like war town misspelled into R&R / feels like white men like this doctor say *maganda* to you, in the lobby, in the street, walking to the grocery store with tank top on and you are only 12 yrs. old / feels like the notion of Spam as nostalgia doesn't apply when it's easy to carry protein in a can when you flee military checkpoints / feels like nanny with other people's children on hip / feels like nanny means someone to fuck with when wife and kids are away on day trips / feels like you are lucky we even let you live here / feels like nose to tail eating isn't as savage when white people sit at communal tables in candlelight / feels like their nurse is hand job / feels like their massage therapist is hand job / their care aid is hand job / feels like they are devoutly catholic, fear god, so essentially fear white people / feels like my outer layer open, exposed, my medical treatment relies on this moment / feels like hipdeep dank dysphoria / feels like too many emotions hung on the laundry line / feels like when the doctor tells you about the ocean, you know y'all don't have the same cultural reference point / feels thirsty, please give me water to get a moment alone / feels like another white man at some reading who talks to you about water torture when you were talking about tanka poems / feels like tanks again, in your dreams, dreams of your lola, inheritance / feels like stethoscope, clipboard, MRI / feels like you are seen right through as invisible / feels like you get why mama carried rosary at all times / feels like if there weren't a needle taking my blood, I would say / feels like hunt and cleaver even before the scalpel is mentioned / feels like they steal me out of body / feels like not just about blood samples / feels like theft is killing me.

I just want dimsum undisturbed by wypipo

you googled "authentic" / & now are seated next to me. /
as I speed walk you to the cart / aunty gives me the last dish /
gets the idea that I've waited too long / for something to just
taste right. / I wish for a dumpling stuffed / of bullet skins to
be the shrapnel / in every white man's throat. / go ahead / say
the word oriental / at my table / one more time.

What are alarm clocks when I got spasms?

Chronic pain wakes them up,
guaranteed. It's not all physical.
Some things deeper than bone.
Some rumbles take years to unravel.
Some ache storms under the sinew,
makes residence under your skeleton,
makes long dragging. An erasure.
A dwindling? The thing where you
feel like a visitor in your own flesh.
That, that is what I
mean.

How one might've behaved from ages 19 to 23

when she tossed out hips, there, earthquake,
or maybe my heartbeats were a chorus of drums
praising the choreography of her curve.
either way, make no mistake, we obviously equal tension.
I want to delete the rulers, the scales, tell
her the only weight you deserve is sinking down on teeth,
sashay of fingernails as fierce and as soft as sunrise wind.

we who want pinned wrists and
stretched out mouths upturned like vagabond stars.

we who are one part earth and one part fire,
only lava can take place here.

we want ransack. dislocated lamps, sprained countertops
on blister of our back and forth, we want to pound skin
into a luscious rhythm, the kind of sounds only
the psyche of summer can admit to.

she says, *I like it rough* and I want the wind knocked out of you
not from brute force but by jab of verb
when your body splits into the mattress.

she says *I like it rough.* I picture palm to palm clutched,
I want to make our veins same syncopated beat, she says *I like it rough*
and I say… *okay*
        (thank you universe, unicorns, lesbian jesus christ)
which is to say that we are two brown kids
carnal with buckets of blood that just want to
paint a good picture for once.

buckets which sounds like the term bakit,
and in tagalog which means "why?"
which then suggests, why not *us?*

by now, you can only imagine
what I would say if
we were naked.

because naked I would cross-stitch
your smile and you would leave,
bend over vessel wide, yet walk away as soon as
I reminded you how warrior you could get.

because naked I'd show you kulintang curve
and balisong slice, all with our tongues
but without any words

so I just tell you
        that I want to know your moan.

so I just tell you
        that your lungs can unfold like maps
        if you let me find my way to you.

because writing about skin is only façade.
for we might contort this into ballad
we both aren't ready for.

instead, coax an argument of coast to coast,
it would get too expensive,
all the travel, too far, we're too far.

truth:
ain't no pressure to use the word "love" here.
we all know we've sieved juice from the syllables
already and that gets even the best of us nowhere.
besides, you like alcohol and love the burn down your throat
and I just think of it as poison. this is one of the cons I wrote
down on a list that makes us impossible.

funny, I did not write down your girlfriend's name.

If we are looking for a poem of morals, the
poem you refuse to let me write as it would
only end with your vertebrae,
a ceremony of kissing,

a downbeat of rules snapping,
a list of tabletops we'd tip over with food & fondling,

where our lust would be anything but a weapon.
where our lust would have caused broken hearts,
not excluding our own.

don't ask questions,
keep talking,
my nerves can handle your blaze,
and at least,
thank goodness,
we've always got that.

Tatlo: three

I just want softness on my mouth
For my favorite air sign

But fuckbois come in all shapes   she tells me, which feels
like *don't touch that stove top, it's too hot.* And I won't
repeat what else my friend said, but it was enough to remind
me of my worth, lift me up, be buoy from the basic I keep
trying to—well, that's the problem, isn't it? I keep trying.
Over breakfast, I have this talk, I bite my toast, hope for
consistency, but gesture a crust as she shakes her head,
as I try to find something soft, something yolky, something
like pillow, something like velvet. I guess that's my issue,
I just want softness on my mouth. My younger self didn't
get soft, but sporadic. Patches of love. Scatter of fingers on
chest. Smatter of solace. The mathematics were never right
& if I've learned anything, one can't thrive on the irregular.
Maybe it's an earth sign thing? But fuck, if I could just smell
your hair everyday. Okay, it is an earth sign thing, but I think
what I want to say is that when your hot breath in the LA night
made music on cheek, I thought we could land on something
more than mattress.

+

I thought we could sink into stellar. When you leaned in
it gleamed, you made me a believer, something of substance
could come of us. Not this. Not head nod in hallway.
Not cavern for clarity. Some dead-end Drake song. Some
end that wasn't even a rumble, not a brawl. Not that I want
a fight, just the sweaty part afterwards where we make
up with our limbs, all infinity shapes in surrender. I guess,
my love for you is nothing like food, metaphor doesn't make
due. A week later, here's what I know: you poured so much
on me so fast, I forgot how to drink anything else.

How to make salabat

Hoy! Listen,   *this is how to cut ginger, it's a root,* she said from
Chicago basement on the first snow of the year. It's the 90's.
Snow is a big deal. Tear salt missing ocean salt, she cleared her throat.

Based on where we're from, nothing can prepare us for frozen.
Fast forward: college friend asks *How do you make that tea again?*
The one you used to drink when it started to snow.   I want to say truths:

*My ma is dead. She made this every time it began to snow. I buried both
my parents by age 25. Have you called your mother? Have you checked to
see if there is a tumor slowly living under her skin? What I recall most was*

her crying.   Which is a lot like making any drink really, a pouring,
which reminds me of something a writer friend once mentioned —
If you only write about crying and death nobody will buy your books,

scratch that, maybe I said that to myself? Okay, that isn't inaccurate
per se: how selling books isn't a priority. What I really do is listen to the same
voicemail over and over where my mother's throat is miles away, mouthful

of liquid, steeped tea bags for lungs, just waiting for the right time to let go.
What I actually want to say all the time: Grief is the full-time job.
What I say to my friend only mentions directions — Which leads one to think

about when my mother finally moved back home, *a visit,* she coined it,
vacation, which was code for *for good.* Two weeks later she says in calling
card staccato, *I'm in bad shape, anak.* Which is migrant code for death.

Words have multiple meanings. My mama taught me that. In essence, she
was my first poetry instructor. This is how a mother tongue is whittled dull,
abandoned building, once a home. When the mother dies, you couldn't say that

phrase for years, couldn't say   *she's dead.* How in three languages,
you don't have words for absence. A mouth becomes thud.
English becomes harder to swallow. Did you know, on the worst days

you forget what her favorite song was but the tiny eruption
of her cough repeats   in loop   all the time now?

You + Me = Anomoly
sponsored by T.S.A.

On the fifth city, almost every city, TSA dumps out
all your belongings. Your journal tumbles to the floor,
all your poetry coats the tile. All your hard work.

An agent screams loudly, *Anomaly! We've found an anomaly.*
Do you want a Female or Male agent to search you?
Her tenor spills over much like your stuff. What once
was organized and beautiful is now ransacked mess.

You've become what cis white middle america fears,
something truly Other, unidentifiable, the breath between
boxes, beyond. *Female or Male*   she demands again.

She explains where her hands will go, if I have pain
on my body. I say solemnly, look her in the eye,
Pain is everywhere. It hurts everywhere.

Of course, in standard procedure, presumably cis
suited white men zoom past. *Do you want to be*
searched in plain sight or enclosed room? Plain sight
I mumble. I lock eyes with a brown Sikh man who's
                    also being searched. Our faces focused, we raise arms
                              up in unison like two birds frozen, as
                                  white strangers' hands touch skin
                              and sacred under some guise of freedom.

                    After we each nearly miss boarding times, we are
                    cleared. I ask him if he's okay. He shakes his head,
                    You? I look down like maybe I've got answers, but
                    nothing comes. We apologize to one another for this
           system that scans our bodies until we're checked out of skin.

                    We agree, we never get used to this.
                    You're reminded who you are equals threat—
                              not person, real, or worthy.

           News announcements of Trump's inauguration

splay orchestral music. Horns sound loudly.
Before we rush to our respective gates, we
lock eyes again on the tv monitor.

The bombast of music persists. Both our faces fallen
as we keep watch, hold breath,
without a word, together, in tears.

when we're the only brown people at nomwah

diaspora love is to say, meet me on mott st., turn on doyers st., and wait in line for half an hour. ok. maybe an hour. don't touch each other, but plan what dumplings to eat. don't say a thing, but talk about hand pulled noodles, order two steamed pork buns, one for now, and another for later after we build a real appetite. watch one another pull apart soft dough made by women's hands right at sunrise. before that, i'm in a meeting where a white lady tells me how i don't even sound filipino. before that, you are not thanked for the ways you do all the work among men. we read the headlines and see bodies like ours but never hear our names pronounced correctly, if ever. all our people clean the houses or build the buildings or bake the bread, and we should be so grateful for this immaculate booth, upholstered in red, so grateful for the diplomas, and the crying between airport gates, see how we've made it. i send money back home without envelopes now. you go back to harlem, translate papers to parents. my mouth waters over chive parcels as you reach for the greens, chopsticks pick apart piles of leaves from stems as they sit in the salt of oyster sauce. we talk shop. we claim our worth. together, we order more chili oil and think, this chili oil is hot?—we rub our bellies under the table, still hungry, and smile as if to mean, y'all ain't tasted anything yet.

Pantoum for recital when my mom said, don't let them see you cry

as a child, I was dressed as a bumblebee, buzzing—
on stage, moved to music, the only brown child
at the entire recital, there I was, glowing.
I was taught to be a consummate performer!

on stage, moved to music, the only brown child
still, I knew all the steps, harmonized my muscles,
I was taught to be a consummate performer.
once, I was shoved into the orchestra pit.

still, I knew all the steps, harmonized my muscles.
there, my stinger broken, determined, I crawled out of the hole.
once, I was shoved into the orchestra pit,
all the white girls seemed to laugh with the crescendo.

there, my stinger broken, determined, I crawled out of the hole.
at the entire recital, there I was, glowing.
all the white girls seemed to laugh with the crescendo!
as I child, I was dressed as a bumblebee, buzzing—

when your aunty is lost,
she tries to find you

1.

When my ma was alive we would
talk about our food. How rice
sticks to gums, what oil does
to an onion, how eating feels better
than anything we knew, even better
than how we treated each other
our whole lives.

2.

My Auntie Yoly stuck around long after ma died. Five years after.
In a house that asks *How come you have no boyfriend?* more than
salutations, this woman complimented every haircut like her smile for sea air.
Head with a lightning bolt, side shave like tsunami shimmy, she praised it all.

As she aged, she faced loss of time, a slouched memory, would say
the month was February when it was September. Her heart stuck
somewhere in replay 1995, Logan Square Chicago, the Bulls always
in a championship. Upon her asking, *Kumusta na, anak?*
I want to tell her not all of us survived.

3.

When she asks for my cousins who haven't called
in years, I coo in faux-confidence,
> *They will be here soon*

Not   they assemble rifles like the ones you fled
        they are married to white men
        they do not include your last name on any document

It is clear I do not have the grit of star seams. I don't sway
gentle like the palm leaves of my people. Even though I have
lived here my whole life, I do not have even enough American
in my body to say this.

4.

One afternoon it was my turn:

- Change her clothes
- Wipe her body
- Watch her fumble
- Remind her it's okay
- Who knows what the it is,
  so speak vaguely in soft tones

5.

In an empty room, she touches my hand,
holds it like a nest would an egg, doesn't move.
Comfort feels like everywhere.

Aunty calls me Cecilia, a ghost name (my mother's name),
syllables harder than the gracious Saint from which it came.

6.

Be good to her, anak.
     Your child.   *Kay* (my name) *doesn't*
                                   mean anything,

she's just as
     rebellious as you were.
          You cannot blame her for that.

Tell her—
     You miss her.
Tell them—

     They can come
     home now.

Princess Urduja: an Exclusive Interview

"DAGUPAN CITY—This beautiful princess was so strong and brave that she did not need a dazzling prince to carry her off to his castle. The existence of Princess Urduja, the female warrior depicted in several paintings and after whom the Pangasinan governor's house is named, continues to spark debates. Mar 5, 2017."

Take my blade, for instance. It's speed is wind-fast and that's what
matters to me—Don't tell me a woman cannot fight,

you'll be made a fool like all bodies under my heel
for taking what isn't theirs.

If you think the land can be stolen, look—
if my sword won't get you, this ocean will eat you,
smack your maw open, you think salt stings?

Listen, I am the governor of the port, my seaweed dries
only to the sun. My voice as sharp as steel song in my hands.

When people think of princesses I hope
I make them re-consider.

My dreams split femurs.
My laurels are made of bones.
My multiple tongues make merchants beg for air.
Ask: Are you ready to kill for your people?

If the answer is No, understand warriors
can feel blood break skin easy like breath,
but it doesn't make it any easier. No such thing as an easy kill.
That's a lie you're told.

To take the soil back to its people
is a parting gift. I accept it,
all the of terms—my lost legacy,

even when
        you are free
and don't recognize
my name.

The Get Well Lexicon

after Darlene Laguna

//

the   findings

show

looking at

the   x-ray

you   will note

multiple

gray masses

in   the   joints

subchondral   cysts

also   known as,

a geode.

//
the doctor
was hopeful
and explained

things. doctor
said it is
painful

but there are
more treatments
now

not like twenty
years ago.
I am lucky!

//

Thank you for sending texts, friend.
Thank you for keeping us updated.
What's the treatment plan?
Thank you for the update.
Thanks.
Whew! I thought it would be worse.
I'm here with you.
Thank you for the update!
I appreciate you for keeping us updated.
Dear _____, that sucks! I'm sorry!
Oh, I'm glad. At least doctor was nice?
Thank you for your communication.
Keep us posted.
[frown face emoticon]
[heart emoticon]
[heart emoticon]

//

Must be nice to not work.
You'll get better soon.
The pain can't be forever.
Haven't seen you in a long time.
I miss you.
I miss you.
[Message read]
[Message seen]
[Delivered]
. . .

I only write in Garamond

for Jasmyne

Secret: When I write you poems, I only write in Garamond. Let letters stretch out,
languid & loose, like the way our bodies do when we stay in bed long after noon,

or so I imagine. By phone you said *Times New Roman is trash*. Immediately,
I wanted to call you lover in my language, chart peninsula on your
cheekbones, ask if you had more demands for me.

Ask: Are you ready for this syntax? Long lines I want to write you, the way I scribble
stanzas in the middle of subway stops, urgent, necessary, crowded by emotions.

Love can be stern & easy—I appreciate that reminder from you. Together,
we confess: dusk is our favorite time of day, steak should be eaten rare,
the movie *Hook!* is cinematic genius, because it's a sacred thing to watch

when your gender has never had an answer, but here is an example: Rufio, sword
buckling, long earring adorned, leader. I laugh of pettiness, say something like

how the actual actor is a trash poet. I wonder what you think, how easily I can
throw away my own, another Filipino made into fantasies written by white hands.

If you'll still love me in this constant anger, this quick bitter, my own fists only
undone for your cheeks. If I close my eyes, I imagine the slow tilt of your forehead

on my shoulder as we watch movies on the couch. Us dreaming in one luscious
breath, us moonlit & flying, hand-in-hand, our own adventures soaked in stardust.

Night ends with our limbs swooped like tree branches, still, braided, quietly
growing. Our exhales the up slope swoon of a letter, expanse exquisite,
longing for journey beyond running, planes, gates about to close, just us

together in loop, traveling and writing—going to places we never imagined,
places we never ever thought we could go.

Embrace the future, right?

Single mama stealth means hash browns and mcmuffin cut in halves
or thirds like how magicians split a body. We hope this'll be enough

to feel whole or at least trick our bellies. Grease blood, grease napkins,
grease tongue among babies turned grown people who are statistics
shamed. Not this meal, not this body, not who you were.

>>

Now, one spends $12 on kale salads in neighborhoods
that aren't Black no more but coffee shop plays hard bass stolen

like everything else. Twenty years from now, haute cuisine
of breakfast foods will be taken in pill form, cholesterol froth, a side

kitsch of poverty that everybody used to hate and now recalls
romantically like the of touch ex-lover. Nostalgia = main squeeze.

>>>

Bearded white men in flannel spacesuits will cite trap
music in their thesis. What used to be a bus stop breakfast treat

is heralded as a time before the presidents came after
all of us. Before the chickens with two heads, chills

of snow in May, nuclear stench made communities huddle
under neon green sky. Store clerks will tell kindergarteners

as they fly on their way to school that the taste of potatoes was
more than salt. Ketchup will be a thing of the past. Fondly,

only the richest will have a special bottle kept in pantry quarters.
Its sugar will be on museums shelves. Alien, acidic, something

they tell grandkids about as they sip clouds of resin at dinner
tables. The forks and knives shrug luster, mere decorations.

>>>>

A mother will scold via charcoal filtered mask:
Eat your vegetables. Yes, yes. It's just a saying,
but you know what I mean.

My cousin serves our country

When I hear anything resemble *Buck!Buck!* I drop to the floor, instantly.
Memory charges threat in Upper Eastside to Humboldt Park. Given the right
phone card, Quezon City, Manila. Once I heard a boom in college, in
Lincoln Park, at a party on the first floor. Me and my bestie almost

kissed the fucking ground in a rich-ass brownstone. I come from kinda shaky
& sacred, but my cousin stationed in VA. Pretends she don't know that sort of
sound. Funny, on the phone now, all she talks about is owning property: house,
picket fence, having children, and *What exactly do poets do?*
What do you own?

Not land, I say. My voice. The cackle of our grandparents, I want to say.
A count of paces to the gravestone of your mother. Instead, what comes is*:*
How often do you see your child? Do you even remember what your mama's
laugh sounds like when you're on tour? When was the last time you
visited her grave? She spoke to you in tagalog mostly, remember? I almost say.

I hold back. While I spat poems on scholarship, she watched her battalion
spew up jewels of blood, still dreams about it. Metal, barrel, click, she can
assemble an automatic rifle fast, as fast as school yard pinners, speedy like
metallic smell on her fingertips, like resin wafted in our neighborhood

when a body, face down, boy's hair turned tributary on concrete—she just
started middle school, I was but a sophomore. Fingers are supposed to cover
eyes for surprises like birthday parties. Not this. My palm draped over her pupils,
her cheek pressed to my chest, until our parents came back from night shift.

Brown people have only two choices: be in front of the barrel or behind it.
Something about the body memory. How we both remember iron scent,
like bones of the 1960s remodel on some compound she now sends in
Christmas newsletters: house, children, husband, robin's egg

aluminum siding, matching sweaters, proud flag in the background.
These faces, all smiles, arms wrapped over, like tarp over triage, arms wrapped
hovering, make tent, cover up something we never seem ready to talk about.

The groove of Tito Bong

"The groove is so mysterious we're born with it and we lose it
and the world seems to split apart..."
— Lynda Barry

On the weekends during lunch,
a cigarette balanced on a grin,
BBQ marinade of RC cola, B96 blaring bass,
Tito Bong made the meat.

       Other days, he would call collect,
       tired, broke, she left me
       —he would croon, somewhere
       jukebox, somewhere a speaker

like a cough, reached for air.
Tito, a grown man brown, mud
thick arms, bull of a face, softened
when girl cousins dressed him

       up in lace, mama's best avon lipstick
       samples, sparkly bullets squiggled on cheekbone.
       While he danced cha cha, they'd dip together
       under summer moon. His sad melted like butter.

Tito had no bed. On the back porch,
next to roaches, he slept on a fold out, beside that,
taped polaroids of his parents waving.
This is right before I left home, he'd say.

       We would peak through the screen door,
       watch him dance alone, beer bottles
       a chorus behind, as if to wail was so simple.
       At the same time as he rested, he was still on the way

out. Harmonies hummed him to snores,
the tape deck digging holes the size
of his heart. Also, the groove.

Also, the give up. Also, he always

       knew all the words to every song
       —the dance this country
       made him do
       made him ghost

Apat: four

Loving in the Apocalypse Years

1.

When friends mention
ravaging, it's not bumpy faith.
Now, headlines lacquer our skin,
Courtrooms do as they always do, pillage.
On TV, channels construct:
>   boy
>   woman
>   child
>   sister
>   mother
>   many children
>   many bodies
>   women
>   many
>   many

     The body count is at twelve now as of June 2018,
trans women, brown black skins, we've got another altar,
street corners made constellations all the while.

     They hold up big flags and bellinis,
drink corporate sponsorships like vitamins,
vacay packages and muscled pecs,
tan lines in the Gayest cities,
as many as chalk lines on the concrete.
None of this is our land.

2.

Today:
>   my student texted me shaking
>   my lover woke up cracking throat into screams,
>   her arm always at pills length
>   my client rocks back and forth, *they are going to deport my parents*
>   my sibling seizes tremors at the SSDI office,
>   hasn't written a stanza in weeks

my mother whimpers in her grave
    hopes this world gets its shit together
my father, dead in a podunk cemetery & a court
    refuses the pollution that killed him

why does the sound of laughter have a bullet behind it?
why does a fist, just the circumference of the heart, now hold its hackles up?
how can this universe be a pillow and not a landmine?
what ways do I make my soul a swallowing and a shield?

3.

Please just tell us
how do
we stay
afloat
when I am too busy
stockpiling canned goods
trying to build
a shelter

of
everyone
I meet?

Why I don't go to bars with white poets anymore

when you are alone
the crowd chants
like they
are some revival.
a skinny white
person licks lips
and you wonder why this
makes you quiver
not in warm welcome,
but the kind that
has you looking over
your shoulder,
like your last bite
like your last dollar
like your last idea
like you can't miss
a moment
or else
it'll get ganked
and sold.

she stands on top of the
table with rage.
like every white woman I've met,
like *she* was spat on,
like there was a metaphorical
bottle that made snap
crackle of her popped eyelid.
the sign in her hands reads
Only Men and Women Here
as it crumples into the white
palm. sometimes you don't
believe in signs and you
can't trust the people
who shout the loudest either.

you say nothing.
think of your safety

in a room of 100 white people
your skin as Brown
as the bar light
you are the only person
whose pronouns are
barbwire on smooth
tongues at wine and cheese
poetry readings. to make a
ruckus means an emotional
vacay for others who
have more than enough
to pay rent, to likely own anything.

funny, cuz strangers choke
on chardonnay before you
share your name,
shake a hand,
but well intentions
mean that direct actions
only happen when
you can afford to not flinch
at the podium
poetry reading
where claps
are broken drums

next to another
sign that reads
    keep your belongings close,
    we are not responsible
    for any theft
    or lost personal
    items.

Princess Urduja before the battle that killed her

Last night, for ritual, I considered collecting your blood and hair on my pillow,
making a net as transparent as fish tail, follicles thin as sewing pins. I harvested
your aches, built hope for you in twilight, on each new moon. Which is likely
part of the problem—every cycle, I fight for you. Pose questions for you.
All this, when I am shell song longing for the sound of answers.

This is the way of a woman warrior; time should do something about that.
I collect in candlelight: slope of our first karabao horn, sampaguita petals,
sand silt, fallen coconut shell, scars like underbelly of boats,
still with merchants stealing, absence. I award myself a cadence of change,

my heart never becomes fist, I save that for battles aged into wars. For you,
I take herb to fingertip, praise metal as last song. Make my body
highest tide to kiss a crescent moon, love you not knowing my name
will be apparition. In the future, what once was a riverbed where I swung

weapons will be a mall where my people flee during storm season. Scholars will
hold symposium over my name. Long hours dedicated to But, did she even exist?
Again, ignorance messes with expectations of woman warriors, our strength
misread as imperceptible. There will be a monument of me carved in slate

near school children in uniforms who sip up sweet things from straws.
They'll know me as meeting place, forever my hands full of sword, body frozen
mid-fight. Which is something I try to accept. I'd rather become someone's
dream or resting place. I'd rather my varnish be a myth than a failure.

For Brandon

William Brandon Lacy Campos (August 31, 1977 — November 9, 2012)

When you hugged me, I circled my palm
on thick flesh of your chest, gave it an extra second.
You never know the last time you get to love on
somebody ever, but it was obvious to me to
feel honored.

In the West Village, I read a draft of a poem to you
during Monday all-you-can-eat crab special
as we unfolded bibs and got ready for mess.

There's a photo of this time,
each dimple of yours like sparklers on a Midwestern night,
a red orange cartoon plastic crustacean waves
over your pecs, protection from splatters.

I imagine your heartbeat a buffet
for proper eardrums. It reminded me
that there were other dreamy men
who weren't worthy. But,
here I was.

Together, an afternoon meant we slid sinew,
slurped joints to get to substance.
In tears, I would summon my dead mama
and you would erupt over a
buttery claw on how we learned
to eat this way,
       by our mama's
      mama's mama,
           the both   of us.

What I remember is that you cried too, probably
about another friend you've lost.
Why does the world take away the good ones?

Still, we cackled and went on for hours,
feeling fed, feeling like at least we have
handfuls of something now,

at least we are the ones at the end here,
not broken.

Later that afternoon you texted,
      OMG ading, my lips are burning.
      I think I am allergic to Old Bay

and I sent an
      LOL me too?
and told you
      OH NO! I love you. #Twins
            (heart emoji, waves emoji, flame emoji)

We never got to meet up after that.
I saved this text, to hold onto the nuance—
the kinship of hunger and pain
so big, you want to laugh.

In my mind, you eat
everything that is everything.
There's a dance floor with a DJ who must
be somebody's trusted cousin from up the block

and there is no blood spilled anywhere.
In my dreams, there is not shame
for a body however sick or queer or brown.

There is not living or dead
and you are still with us,

face moist from strobe lights,
voice raucous in loudspeakers' scream:

We have poems, we have liberation,
we have homes, we have medicine,
we have each other
indefinitely.

Tell a child about something
that causes you fear or dread
with gratitude to Samiya Bashir

It's ok to
be just wound
sometimes.

To gape, cry, rock,
shiver, rumble, ramshackle,
shake ancestors in your sleep.

To be part dead.
Razor, lash, hang,
to be the thing that flails,
to be cathedral, to be gravestone.
To speak cobweb.

Let me tell you:
to die everyday is the kind of pulse that makes
music. Be the kid who leans against books
more than people. Be the book as it opens,
closes, folds in on itself, on the same
paragraph. Be the underlined stanza
whose body bursts syntax scars naked.

Love body when it emblazons family curse,
when you are bad joke at the table,
when you are shuffled scrapes of
forks, the weirdo told shut up,
forsaken.

Let lonely make a lens so clear you become intergalactic.
Let residue be a blanket you shed every season.
Let your gaze be salve & sign of the cross.
Let you be words a stranger waits for.
Let love be a bunker you crawl into.
Let you guffaw, let you cackle.
Let you be last one left.
Let you be last one.
Let you be last.
Let you be.
Let you.
Let.

What I learned after moving

with gratitude for Rhoda Rae Gutierrez

Dear Rhoda,
Sometimes I do what you did for me—
open up my home,
give someone the keys, let them
raid the fridge. I'll say
There's bone broth,
Here's the longanisa,
Don't bother with the dishes,
         like a real grown up!

        *

Dear Rhoda,
When I said I left the Midwest for poetry,
I meant I was closer to the ocean now
and in all ways closer to drowning,
but mainly, I just wanted to enter a force
bigger than whatever I grew up with.
What I don't bother to tell you
is admittedly, I give myself
a slow death every day,
something mundane enough like
not brushing my teeth at night.

        *

Dear Rhoda,
Remember that time we didn't
even know each other, before
big city dreams, off the Redline
Argyle stop? We went to a restaurant,
pointed to a brute of a photo,
and ordered the biggest garlic dungeness crab.
This was before the dead mom,
the frantic burial,
me crying in the living room,
your hand pressed on every exhale.
In a mentor, you want someone who
can dig through the cracks,

someone unafraid of splinter,
someone who can find grace
in the pungent, meat under the nails,
still with a grin like a sunset.

*

Well, what is almost as good as that?
I now live in a wave of people,
up to the ears in emotions.
Empathy on the C train
is a thing, therefore
one cries about never
belonging anywhere, which is
what actually makes a true
New Yorker, or at least
a tolerable transplant.

*

Thanks to you,
in a different area code,
when the empty house
becomes pages on the floor,
I cook myself something
from the Atlantic,
to remember us.
Something
that needs both hands.
And I let myself feed,
what could be considered sloppy.
I think undulation,
I think don't be afraid
to let the steam rise,
allow this craving,
the kind of cause
that makes a person
want to lay down
and just
live in it.

Acknowledgments & Gratitude

Thank you to my political, cultural work, and support community, namely:
Geleni Fontaine, Lissette Cheng, Rhoda Rae Gutierrez, Jasmyne Hammonds, Bamby Salcedo, Ann Russo, Francesca Royster, Keiko Wright, Kathy Zhang, Bilen Berhanu, Prerna Sampát, Bri Moore, Ro Garrido, Karen Hanna, Jim Andralis, Pam Nuchols, Darlene Torres, Suzy Salemi, Jim Andralis, Andre Leneal Gardner, Rushaan Kumar, Akemi Nishida, Bev Romero, Aemilius Ramirez, zaynab shahar, Ejeris Dixon, Elliott Fukui, Giselle Buchanan, Jess X. Chen, Kit Yan, Melissa Li, Cristy C. Road, Gabriel Foster, Sheltreese McCoy, Tina Vaden, Maya Gittelman, Grace Piper, Phoebe Connelly, Patrick Balthrop, Tova Leibowitz, Jessica Halem, Jay Toole, Sarah Zia, Sami Schalk, Denise Brown, Eli Clare, Diana Doty, Sage Crump, Deborah Kodish.

To my poetry and writing family:
Samiya Bashir, Sharon Bridgforth, Brandon Lacy Campos, T.C. Tolbert, Kirin Khan, Sokunthary Svay, Lani Montreal, Tanea Lunsford Lynx, Medjulene Shomali, Devi Laskar, Sabrina Ghaus, Shirley Kim Ryu, Zahra Noorbakhsh, Ramy El-Etreby, Amir Rabiyah, Mary Ann Thomas, Amanda Torres, Ydalmi Vanessa Noriega Perez, Jubi Arriola Headley, Celeste Chan, Aldrin Valdez, Pamela Sneed, Rajiv Mohibir, Joseph Legaspi, Cyree Jarelle Johnston, Lisa Factora-Borchers, Anita Dolce Vita, Ryka Aoki, Oliver Baez Bendorf, Sherwin Bitsui, Dane Edidi Figueroa, Addie Tsai, Angela Peñarendo, Muriel Leung, CB Lee, Carsen Bekar, Brandon Som, JT Tamayo, Vidhu Aggarwal, Amanda Torres, Martina Downey, Tawanna Sullivan, Nico Amador, Sue Landers, William Johnson, Edxie Betts, Jade Martinez, Natalie Sharp, Trace Peterson, CA Conrad, Miles Collins-Sibley, Kayla AE, Whitney Porter, Maurisa Thompson, Jesse Rice-Evans, Jordan Franklin, Annie Mok, Darlene Laguna, Jen Soong, Ashna Ali, Natasha Dinnerstein, Nancy Au, Carlos Sirah, Kiyan Williams, Marcello Hernandez Castillo, Jennifer Cox, Rachel Mennies, Nora Whelan, Hanna Ensor, Haili Graff, Bryan Borland, Seth Pennington.

Some of these poems were written with the support of the following resources:
Lambda Literary Review Foundation, VONA/Voices of a Nation, Macondo Writers Workshop, Poetry Foundation + Crescendo Literary, The Home School, Poets In Need, Transjustice Funding Project.

Poems previously published in various forms in the following:
Academy of American Poets, The Advocate, American Studies Journal, Apogee, Asian American Literary Review, BITCH Magazine, Cosmonauts Ave., Entropy, fields magazine, f(r)iction, Fog Lifter, Make/shift, The Margins, Deaf Poets Society, Nat.Brut, NYLON, The New York Times, PBS News Hour, Platypus Press, Poets House, Split This Rock, TAYO Magazine, them., Queer Asian Contemporary Art, VIDA Review.

Gratitude to the following venues for making homes for my works:
Lincoln Center, Asian American Writers Workshop, Poets House, The Poetry Project, Symphony Space, Queens Museum, Asia Arts Initiative, The Leeway Foundation, The Hemispheric Institute, Duke University Center for Documentary Studies, Tucson Poetry Festival, The Dodge Poetry Foundation, The School of The Arts Institute, The U.N.

The Poet

Named one of *9 Transgender and Gender Nonconforming Writers You Should Know* by *Vogue*, KAY ULANDAY BARRETT aka @Brownroundboi is a poet, performer, and cultural strategist. K. has featured at The Lincoln Center, The U.N., Symphony Space, Princeton University, Tucson Poetry Festival, NY Poetry Festival, The Dodge Poetry Foundation, The Hemispheric Institute, and Brooklyn Museum. They are a two-time Pushcart Prize nominee, Best of the Net Split This Rock 2019 nominee, and a 2019 Queeroes Literary Honoree by *Them.*+ Condé Nast. They received fellowships and residencies from Lambda Literary Foundation, VONA/Voices, Monson Arts, and Macondo. They have been Guest Editor for *Nat.Brut* & Guest Faculty for The Poetry Foundation. They have served on boards and committees for the following: The Audre Lorde Project, Transgender Law Center, Sylvia Rivera Law Project, The Leeway Foundation, Res Artis, and the TransJustice Funding Project. Their contributions are found in *American Poets, The New York Times, Buzzfeed, Asian American Literary Review, PBS News Hour, Race Forward, NYLON, The Huffington Post, Bitch Magazine,* and more. Their first book was *When The Chant Comes* (Topside Press). *More Than Organs* (Sibling Rivalry Press) is their second collection. Currently, Kay lives outside of the NYC area with his jowly dog and remixes his mama's recipes whenever possible.

www.kaybarrett.net

The Press

Sibling Rivalry Press is an independent press based in Little Rock, Arkansas. It is a sponsored project of Fractured Atlas, a nonprofit arts service organization. Contributions to support the operations of Sibling Rivalry Press are tax-deductible to the extent permitted by law, and your donations will directly assist in the publication of work that disturbs and enraptures. To contribute to the publication of more books like this one, please visit our website and click *donate*.

Sibling Rivalry Press gratefully acknowledges the following donors, without whom this book would not be possible:

Anonymous (18)
Arkansas Arts Council
John Bateman
W. Stephen Breedlove
Dustin Brookshire
Sarah Browning
Billy Butler
Asher Carter
Don Cellini
Nicole Connolly
Jim Cory
Risa Denenberg
John Gaudin
In Memory of Karen Hayes
Gustavo Hernandez
Amy Holman
Jessica Jacobs & Nickole Brown
Paige James
Nahal Suzanne Jamir
Allison Joseph
Collin Kelley
Trevor Ketner

Andrea Lawlor
Anthony Lioi
Ed Madden & Bert Easter
Mitchell, Blackstock, Ivers & Sneddon, PLLC
Stephen Mitchell
National Endowment for the Arts
Stacy Pendergrast
Simon Randall
Paul Romero
Randi M. Romo
Carol Rosenfeld
Joseph Ross
In Memory of Bill Rous
Matthew Siegel
Alana Smoot
Katherine Sullivan
Tony Taylor
Leslie Taylor
Hugh Tipping
Guy Traiber
Mark Ward
Robert Wright

CPSIA information can be obtained
at www.ICGtesting.com
Printed in the USA
BVHW030037020222
627783BV00008B/1792